GAME
PLAN

SOCCER

THOMAS S. OWENS
DIANA STAR HELMER

TWENTY-FIRST CENTURY BOOKS
BROOKFIELD, CONNECTICUT

To Mario and Gustavo Sandoval, Men of Football

Cover photograph courtesy of © Duomo

Photographs courtesy of Allsport: pp. 7 (© Shaun Botterill), 12 (© David Cannon), 22 (© Simon Bruty), 27 (© Tony Quinn), 29 (© Scott Indermaur/MLS), 33 (© Jonathan Daniel), 34 (© Ben Radford), 39 (© Shaun Botterill), 45 (© Olive Brunskill); Reuters/Gary Hershorn/Archive Photos: p. 9; UPI/Corbis-Bettmann: p. 15; Duomo: pp. 18 (© 1977 Steven E. Sutton), 21 (© 1996 Chris Cole), 25 (© 1998 Steven E. Sutton), 31 (© 1998 Chris Trotman), 43 (© 1996 Ben Van Hook); SportsChrome USA: pp. 37 (© Rob Tringali, Jr.), 44 (© Bongarts Photography); Archive Photos: pp. 49 (© Monte Fresco/PPP), 52 (©Dave Joiner/PPP); Popperfoto/Archive Photos: p. 51

Library of Congress Cataloging-in-Publication Data
Owens, Tom, 1960–
    Soccer / by Thomas S. Owens and Diana Star Helmer.
    p. cm.
    Includes bibliographical references and index.
    Summary: Describes the various positions on a soccer team, techniques involved, top players from around the world, as well as World Cup play.
    ISBN 0-7613-1400-8 (lib. bdg.)
    1. Soccer Juvenile literature. [1. Soccer.]
I. Helmer, Diana Star, 1962– . II. Title. III. Series: Owens, Tom, 1960– Game Plan.
GV943.25.094   2000
796.334—dc21

99-41541   CIP
AC

Published by Twenty-First Century Books
A Division of The Millbrook Press, Inc.
2 Old New Milford Road
Brookfield, Connecticut 06804

www.millbrookpress.com

CONTENTS

TWO TEAMS, ONE DREAM

The date was July 4, 1994. The United States men's soccer team wanted to make it a true Independence Day.

They were about to take the field against soccer powerhouse Brazil for the second round of World Cup competition at Stanford Stadium, an arena near San Francisco, California. The stands, often filled with college football fans, swelled instead with 84,177 soccer fans. But the World Cup could not be compared to America's Super Bowl or World Series. For soccer's World Cup is truly a world event, gathering teams from around the globe for a championship held only once every four years.

The event is huge. But in 1994 the U.S. team's plan was modest: to advance at least to the second round of play. The international organization of soccer, FIFA (Federation Internationale de Football Association), had its own game plan: to show American sports fans that soccer deserved the same respect given to that country's four biggest attractions—baseball, basketball, football, and hockey.

That plan seemed to be working: A ticket reseller said public demand for tickets was so high that a choice midfield line seat, originally costing $125, could be resold for $350 to $400. Eight other American cities were set to host games for the monthlong tournament that had begun June 17.

In this 15th World Cup, the U.S. men's national team—one of 24 teams in the 52-game event—achieved its modest game plan. Its opening match against Switzerland ended in a 1–1 tie, thanks to a free kick by Eric Wynalda. Even so, the Americans certainly weren't favored to top talented Colombia in their next game. However, in the fifty-second minute, Ernie Stewart scored following a Tab Ramos chip to give the U.S. the lead. Ramos's arcing assist cleared a forest of Colombian defenders, and the final score of 2–1 electrified a Rose Bowl crowd of 93,869.

Romania dealt the U.S. team a 1–0 loss at the end of first-round play. Still, the Americans had succeeded in their first game plan. They had made the second round of 16 teams. But they would need a new game plan for their next challenge: facing Brazil on July 4.

America was led by coach Bora Milutinovic. Although he had been coaching the U.S. team since March 1991, nonsoccer fans knew little about this well-traveled personality. Born in Yugoslavia, Milutinovic spoke to reporters in Spanish because he had played professionally in Mexico for years. Later, he had returned to coach the Mexican national team to the 1986 World Cup quarterfinals.

In 1994, Coach Milutinovic called for defense, and lots of it, from his Americans. His game plan? To win a scoreless game in overtime or during a penalty-kick shootout.

Slow, cautious play marked the first half. Near the beginning of the game, a cross to America's Thomas Dooley squirted out of bounds close to the goalpost before Dooley could act. But this would be the USA's only attacking opportunity. The Americans didn't manage a single shot against Brazil's goalie, Taffarel.

Blood Sport

Just before halftime, U.S. halfback Tab Ramos fouled Brazilian defender Leonardo, who came back with an elbow to Ramos's head.

The U.S. men's national team celebrates its unexpected 2–1 win over Colombia on June 22, 1994, in the 15th World Cup.

Leonardo was thrown out of the game with a "red card" ejection. Ramos was carried out on a stretcher, with a fractured skull.

Later Ramos would tell reporters: "I heard this noise in my head that was like a train going through and all I thought was like, 'Oh, my God! I'm going to die right here.' I couldn't feel my legs or my arms or anything. I just wanted to keep my eyes open. That's how bad it was."

Because of the red card, Brazil couldn't replace Leonardo. And they still couldn't penetrate the American defense. For 74 minutes, the game remained scoreless until, at last, Brazil's Bebeto scored the only goal of the game. The match ended without a single save for Brazil's goalkeeper: America's focus on defense meant that Team USA did not attempt a single shot.

Mauro Prais, editor of the Internet Web site "Brazil: Land of Football," was in the Stanford stands to witness the match. "The score was close, but the game wasn't," he remembered. "Brazil had several chances to score. The U.S. had none."

According to Prais, Bebeto's goal wasn't Brazil's only offensive break: In the first half, Bebeto almost scored on a half bicycle [kick], and Romario hit the post from long range. "Had Brazil scored in the first half, they would have been able to control their nerves and maybe obtain an easier win," Prais said.

Prais called Leonardo's ejection a "crucial event. With one man down in the second half, Brazil was perturbed and encountered more difficulties." A minute into the half, Prais pointed out, "U.S. defender Alexi Lalas saved on the goal line. Later, Romario faked his way past the goalkeeper and incredibly missed the goal."

USA's Thomas Dooley (left) battles for the ball with Brazil's Mazinho in the second-round match of the World Cup, July 4, 1994.

Taking Chances

Brazilian play "was still dominant in the game," said Prais. But "as time passed and a couple more chances were squandered, even the Brazilian crowd, in minority at the stadium, became very nervous." After all, "It's a relatively common scenario in soccer, when a team attacks [and] attacks and doesn't get to score, they end up being scored against at the end." Even so, Prais believed that "given how the teams were playing, nobody could see a different outcome."

Was America too careful? Prais said that, in the end, American coach Milutinovic "got his second desirable result, which was not to get creamed. The U.S. team was very well organized, but showed at times to have limited skills and experience."

Brazil would end the tournament as World Cup champion, downing Italy 3–2 in overtime in the deciding match. Brazil's assistant coach, Mario Zagallo, explained his team's game plan, the 4–4–2 formation. In this system, players cluster near midfield in a defensive-oriented pattern with 4 defenders, 4 midfielders, and 2 forwards. Zagallo noted that Brazil, Italy, and Sweden, the top three finishers, all chose the same strategy.

"One [team] can use the same system and [still] be different," Zagallo said. "A team can use a 4–4–2 and attack with two men like Italy did, or it can use a 4–4–2 and send five or six men to the attack, including backs and midfielders, taking the game to another level, like Brazil did."

Meanwhile, the game moved to another level in America. What most Americans once saw as a little-known college sport was now an international event. It was a new chapter in American soccer history.

> Professional bookmakers studied the 1994 World Cup teams to determine betting odds for the most- and least-likely teams to win. Favorites Germany and Brazil had the surest odds at 4-to-1, meaning a dollar bet could pay four dollars if those teams won. America's odds of winning were 50-to-1.

THE REAL TEAM LEADER

2

Any soccer team has one person at its root, its core, its heart.

An unstoppable scorer? A ball-eating goalkeeper? No. A team grows from its coach.

A coach must do more than teach skills to players. A coach must be able to judge the existing skills of his players, so he can fit them together on the field like pieces of a jigsaw puzzle.

Sometimes, fitting puzzle pieces is easy. For example, when coaches know which players are left-footed and which are right-footed, they know which side of the field a player would handle the best.

Working a puzzle is more difficult when one of the pieces is missing. In soccer, as in hockey, a player can be ejected for fouls, and the team must continue—shorthanded. In the 1998 World Cup, French coach Aimé Jacquet had to cope without talented midfielder Zinedine Zidane, who was ejected after kicking a Saudi Arabian player in a first-round game. When a suspension followed, France faced tournament elimination against Paraguay. "Zizou, the French team is not just you," Coach Jacquet told his regretful star. "But [I know] that it's you who'll make us win."

Dutch coach Rinus Michels seldom had holes in his puzzle. That's because Michels could make many pictures with the same puzzle pieces. He was the first coach credited with "Total Football," a concept in which every player on a team is capable of playing every position.

Confused over the way some countries call soccer "football?" Then ask about the person running the team. In Europe, the terms "trainer" and "manager" are often substituted for "coach." Same job, three different titles.

Michels led Holland to second-place finishes in the 1974 and 1978 World Cups with this game plan.

Unlike a zone defense, the Dutch game plan was more of a group defense—and offense. Holland's team members could rotate positions. With or without the ball, players were always shifting their locations, constantly surprising opponents.

The most difficult part of this "without-the-ball" game plan was not in getting players to move about, Coach Michels said. "But to get players to do it intelligently—that's the difference."

And players are supposed to execute game plans on their own. Soccer's ruling organization, FIFA, originally allowed no coaching from the

Coach Rinus Michels led Holland to second place in the 1978 World Cup. His game plan called for every player on the team to be able to play every position.

boundary lines. Later, before the 1990 World Cup in Italy, FIFA ruled that coaching was only allowed from the bench. By the 1994 Cup in the United States, FIFA had softened its rules even more. Coaches could be on their feet shouting instructions near a play in progress, but were "supposed" to be seated after they delivered their message. Coaching staffs have become expert at bending such rules to the extreme. For, though soccer is sometimes called "The Simplest Game," coaches may insist they are *never* done instructing players how to play it.

Trying Not to Lose

Innovative coaches are often remembered, even when their teams seem forgotten. In 1947 a first-division Italian League club in Triestina hired Coach Nereo Rocco. He devised a plan called *catenaccio*, an Italian word for a huge chain. The formation could have been called a 1–3–3–3, consisting of 3 defenders, 3 midfielders, and 3 forwards, with a *libero* (meaning "free player" or "sweeper") playing in front of the goal. The libero was free to play where needed on defense. Often, no more than two of the forwards were strikers. Rocco's game plan was not to win games but to *avoid losing* them. And he did so well that other coaches soon copied his game plan.

But even a good thing can go too far. Before the 1998 World Cup, American coach Steve Sampson's game plan encountered many doubters. Sampson's 3–6–1 formation was not attack-minded. Instead, the game plan relied on a stacked-up defense. The hope was to force lots of turnovers, end in a draw, and go for the win in an overtime shootout.

Sampson lost America's opening game to West Germany, 2–0. He kept losing when the game was done. Soccer historian Paul Gardner blasted Sampson's game plan in *USA TODAY.* "A team that lines up with only one forward is clearly not one that has attacking soccer as its

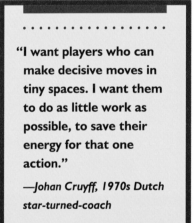

"I want players who can make decisive moves in tiny spaces. I want them to do as little work as possible, to save their energy for that one action."

—*Johan Cruyff, 1970s Dutch star-turned-coach*

main objective," Gardner wrote. "It also simplifies the opposing team's defensive duties." He concluded his report by calling the 3–6–1 formation a "headless chicken."

Sampson's off-field decisions drew criticism, too. Fans wanted to know: Where was John Harkes, the U.S.-born English football star? Famed for his offensive style in England's Premier League, Harkes had returned to play for Major League Soccer in America. Coach Sampson not only made Harkes national team captain in 1994, but he proclaimed him "Captain for Life." So why wasn't Harkes on the 1998 national team? The answer was back in England, where Harkes's efforts on defense were often criticized. That left little room for him in Sampson's defense-based game plan.

Of course, all coaches face criticism for not picking and keeping the best players. But if Coach Sampson's American team hadn't finished last in the Cup competition (32nd among 32 teams), fewer reporters would have questioned Sampson's choice of players. As it was, Sampson finally gave in to widespread pressure to resign.

No Room for Loners at the Top

West Germany's Franz Beckenbauer was the first player to win a World Cup both as a coach and as a player. As a player in the 1974 World Cup, he saw how any given mix of personalities on a team can explode under pressure.

"After three games," Beckenbauer said, the team knew "we played very bad. Then we had a big disaster, a big confrontation—the players, the coaches—everything. We were angry and unhappy. . . . It was almost a fight." Beckenbauer blamed another player, Uli Hoeness. "He was a young star at this time. A lot of abilities and a lot of talent. But he was playing, more or less, for himself. On a national team, there's no one allowed to play for himself."

Franz Beckenbauer (left), coach/player for West Germany, clears the ball in the 1974 World Cup final. West Germany defeated Holland 2–1 to win the championship.

Finally, Beckenbauer said, "We came together as a team. We had a big conversation." And West Germany came from behind to take home the World Cup in a final against the Netherlands, 2–1.

Not surprisingly, when Beckenbauer retired in 1983, his home country wanted him back as a trainer (a European term for coach). He accepted, but told sports federation officials that he wanted to coach for no more than two years. This was enough time, he explained: "How long does it take to get the situation quiet, to bring the belief [in the team] back—from the people, from the press, from everybody?"

Bruce Arena needed his own timetable when he became head coach of the U.S. men's national team in 1998, after Steve Sampson left. Arena's fame began as coach of the University of Virginia, winning the NCAA Division I championship in four consecutive seasons, 1991–1994. He went on to coach D.C. United in Major League Soccer to two championships.

"There's no formula for being successful with talented players," he has said. "It's just how you deal on a daily basis to earn their respect, as the team comes to appreciate what [each] type of player offers."

FAST FORWARD

3

Go forward.

The name says it all. Forwards move that way on the field, with the goal as their usual destination.

A soccer team often uses four forwards. Two strikers play near the midfield. Wingers are positioned outside of strikers. The two wings must be top dribblers and passers, while strikers are the players counted on most for scoring.

But teamwork has to happen in a hurry. Gary Bennett, a striker from England's Premier League, once said, "If you speak to any [goal]keeper, he'll say that the more you dither, the more chance [a goalkeeper has] of standing up to you. So pick your spot and hit it early. That gets [the] best results."

Pelé, often called the "King of Soccer," knew the power of surprise. The star Brazilian forward played in 1,363 matches, scoring 1,282 goals in his 22-year career. And though Pelé did not invent the bicycle kick, he surely perfected it. In executing the bicycle, a player, with his back to the goalie, kicks an airborne ball over his own head toward the goal. The goalkeeper doesn't see the ball appear until the last second, because the player's back blocks sight of the play.

Pelé began as a teenager in a youth league under coach Valdemar De Brito, a star from Brazil's 1934 World Cup team. After three World Cup victories of his own, Pelé joined the New York Cosmos of the North American

Pelé, playing for the Cosmos in 1977, shows his excellent footwork in the last game of his professional career.

Soccer League (NASL) in 1975 for a three-year reign. With his retirement, some soccer fans started thinking that strikers were becoming an endangered species. Pelé knew why attacking soccer was becoming extinct: Offensive players were being beaten up on the field, with few penalties issued. Worse, mass defenses were shutting down even the most creative forwards. Pelé told famed soccer announcer Andres Cantor, "It is ludicrous to see a player go out to the field to entertain the fans, only to become a punching bag."

Changing the Score

The problem wasn't new. When organized soccer began in 1860, rulemakers had debated whether players should be allowed to kick each other!

"These days, you need more and more complete players, because the competition is furious. If you kick with only one foot, your field of action is limited. That's why it's important—it's paramount—to have the ability to kick the ball with each foot. I highly recommend young players to practice different shots and passes with each foot. For example, if you're a forward and if you only manage one side, the defender can forecast what your play will be. On the other hand, you will be able to increase your imagination if your resources let you choose your boundaries, instead of your defender."

—*Emilio Butragueño, who scored four goals for Spain versus Denmark in the 1990 World Cup*

More than a century later, Brazilian midfielder Juñinho, seen as a rising star, suffered a broken leg after being tackled from behind in a league game. At last, FIFA made one of its most radical rules in years: Starting in 1998, *all* tackles from behind would be illegal. (Previously, rulebooks asked referees to punish only "dangerous" blindside tackles!) Under the new rule, back-tacklers faced red-card ejections.

Mass defenses are still used, however, and are one reason that even the greatest strikers seem to have more unlucky streaks than lucky strikes. But the best never give up. In 12 consecutive games before Euro96, the 1996 European Cup championship tournament, England's Alan Shearer was totally scoreless. Yet he ended the tournament leading all scorers for those games. The record enabled Shearer to get a contract worth a whopping 15 million pounds with his hometown's professional team, Newcastle United—the same team that had declined to sign him when he was 14.

Two of the greatest strikers representing the United States in the 1990s were women. Mia Hamm and Michelle Akers were both members of the American team that won the first-ever Women's World Cup in China in 1991. At age 19, Hamm was the youngest member of that team. Teammate Akers collected the "Golden Boot" as top tournament scorer that first year. Although the U.S. women's national team fell to third in the following Women's World Cup in 1995, Akers and Hamm helped win another first-ever gold medal when women's soccer was added to the Olympic games in 1996.

Hamm, whose University of North Carolina team won NCAA championships four years in a row, is famed for her team-first attitude. Along with her reputation for dishing out assists from a traditional scorer's position, she filled in as a midfielder and goalkeeper during the 1995 World Cup.

Hamm and Akers were an important part of America's 1999 Women's World Cup championship. On July 10, 1999, California's sold-out Rose Bowl brimmed with 90,185 fans. TV viewers numbered 40 million. China and the United States remained scoreless after 90 minutes of regulation play and two 15-minute overtimes. The U.S. women won at last, 5-4, during the concluding penalty-kick phase.

Wings Help Offenses Fly

Conventional wisdom holds that strikers are set to score, and wingers are primed for assists. Forwards sometimes share these traditional roles, to better surprise opponents. But tradition works to a winger's favor in the

How did famed U.S. striker Mia Hamm gain her love of soccer? Growing up in Wichita Falls, Texas, her family watched TV broadcasts of games from Mexico. Even though the announcing was in Spanish, Mia quickly understood the language of the game.

Mia Hamm (right) of the U.S. women's national team races for the ball against her Norway opponent in the 1996 Olympics.

time-honored "cross." The best wingers make this play look as pretty as an "alley-oop" pass for a slam dunk in basketball. The winger passes, hoping the ball will "cross" uncontested to the center of the field. One or two teammates dash for the goal, arriving in front of the goal just as the ball arrives. Together: goal!

Veteran British winger Mark Taylor said that for the cross, "you can't pick people out. You've got to know where you're going to put the ball." He adds that knowing the habits of strikers is vital. "If you play with them a certain amount of time, you just know they'll be timing their runs right for you to cross it without lifting your head up. If you lift your head up to see where they are, you've delayed too long. They'll be marked [guarded]."

Jurgen Klinsmann raises the trophy for the Euro96 championship. Germany beat the Czech Republic 2–1.

Wingers like Taylor say nothing about speedy teammates. After all, arriving early for a cross would ruin the play as surely as arriving late.

But success as a forward takes more than skill. Helen Kalithrakas, an Australian fan of West Germany striker Jurgen Klinsmann, described what made her favorite player's 11-year career extraordinary.

"He had passion, positive mental attitude, courage, an excellent temperament and most of all, he was a team player," she said. "A great example of this was in the Euro96 championships in England. For most of the tournament, Klinsmann was plagued by a recurring injury. He missed the first game and, of course, the semifinal game versus England.

"Although he was nowhere near 100 percent fit to play, Klinsmann joined his beloved Germany in the final versus the Czech Republic," continued Kalithrakas. "Klinsmann was visibly in agony out there on the pitch, but it was his mentality that made him last right through till the end, in which Germany overcame them, 2–1."

She remembers more than the final score, which came after 120 minutes and overtime. "Klinsmann's tears of pure ecstasy and joy after the game was a moving experience for me," she said.

Few teams succeed without forwards who score. Yet when France entered its 1998 World Cup final against Brazil, French forwards had remained scoreless in the previous three games.

Kalithrakas was 12 years old when she first saw the West German star play in the 1990 World Cup. She says he inspired her to play soccer and still inspires her, even after his 1998 retirement. Kalithrakas believes that one quote from a 1995 British magazine article sums up her hero's career.

During the height of Michelle Akers's career, she continued playing despite being diagnosed with Chronic Fatigue and Immune Dysfunction Syndrome (CFIDS), a disease that continually drains a person's physical energy.

"To any young kid who wants to be a footballer," Klinsmann said, "I would simply say: Have fun playing football and enjoy the team spirit. That's the right attitude that will bring you pleasure and fulfillment in football."

A forward with forward thinking. What better game plan is there?

4 NO WEAK LINKS

Midfielders are the links, the transitions between offense and defense. Some soccer followers even call them "linkmen" or "halfbacks" because of their dual jobs.

An average of three midfielders are used in most game plans. Some specialize in attacking, some in defending. Some play "two-way." But all help throughout the field, running an average of 10 miles per game.

Johan Cruyff, the 1970s star on Holland's two second-place World Cup finishes, divided time between striker and midfielder. Cruyff learned on the field the philosophy he carried into coaching professional teams such as Barcelona. "Every trainer talks about movement, about running a lot," said Cruyff. "I say, don't run so much. Football is a game you play with your brains. You have to be in the right place at the right moment, not too early, not too late."

American John Harkes has praised how teams like Cruyff's attack together, to create forward momentum. He also speaks from experience, after more than a decade as an offensive-minded midfielder on British teams.

Cobi Jones paired with Harkes in the midfield for America in the 1994 World Cup games. Jones, who was also a member of the 1992 U. S. Olympic team, built his reputation with solid dribbling and assists. Jones has appeared in more than 100 games for the U.S. national team.

Another American midfielder claimed a stunning bit of history in 1998. Kristine Lilly of the U.S. national team played in her record-

Team USA soccer star Kristine Lilly (left) beats China's Jingxia to the ball in the 1998 Goodwill Games.

breaking 152nd international game, tops for any man or woman in the world. "With her work ethic and warrior spirit, Kristine epitomizes the success of not only the U.S. women's national team during its history, but the growth of women's soccer worldwide," said team coach Tony Di-Cicco. "Her creative attacking style makes the women's game highly entertaining, and she has the undying respect of not only her teammates and coaches, but also opponents worldwide."

Give Them a Devil of a Time

World Cup 1998 followers might know Michel Platini only as co-president of the French organizing effort to get the tournament in their country. Yet, before his retirement at age 32, Platini was a star midfielder for the French national team. He won "European Footballer of the Year" honors three times (1983–1985). France made World Cup semifinals with Platini in 1982 and 1986, and won the European Cup in 1984. Platini is remembered for his free-kick talent. He seemed to have the power to direct his kicks around walls of defenders.

Another midfielder captured Most Valuable Player honors in the 1998 Major League Soccer season. Not only that, but Bolivian Marco Etcheverry became the only player ever to make the MLS all-stars in each of the league's first three years. The league's all-time assists leader was nicknamed "El Diablo" as his career began. The star's brother-in-law claimed Etcheverry looked as though he was possessed by the devil whenever he dribbled the ball. Etcheverry was possessed—but only by the desire to win. He took D.C. United to two league titles in three seasons.

Other midfielders stress the defensive part of their game. Sharing a spot with Etcheverry on the MLS "Best 11"

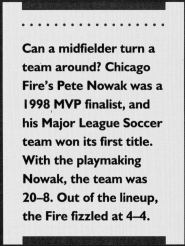

Can a midfielder turn a team around? Chicago Fire's Pete Nowak was a 1998 MVP finalist, and his Major League Soccer team won its first title. With the playmaking Nowak, the team was 20–8. Out of the lineup, the Fire fizzled at 4–4.

D.C. United midfielder Marco Etcheverry is an outstanding dribbler. Here he shows his skill in a 1998 game.

Frankie Hejduk inspired the 1998 U.S. national team as a second-half midfield substitute in World Cup play against Germany. His hustle didn't erase Germany's 2–0 lead, but Hejduk tried everything. He even wore his shorts backward for good luck.

(all-stars) in 1998 was Chris Armas. The Chicago Fire's defensive midfielder was a specialist at marking the opposing, offensive-minded midfielder. When Armas was shutting down attacks, foes often forgot he was only 5 foot 7 and 150 pounds. Armas didn't let opponents forget anything else. He played every minute of Chicago's first 31 games before getting a rest in the last game of the season.

Phil Neville, after logging time in the Manchester United midfield, described one aspect of a defensive midfielder's job. "You don't want to foul people deliberately," he said. "But you have to do what's best for the club at that time."

A Marked Man

Defenses closely mark any midfield scoring threat. But a midfielder who takes such coverage personally puts the whole team at risk. David Beckham of England's national team learned this the hard way during a 1998 World Cup match. Frustrated by Argentina's rough play, Beckham finally kicked midfield opponent Diego Simone after Simone was on the ground. Beckham drew a red-card penalty and was ejected from the game. One man down, his team lost the tied second-round game in the penalty-kick shootout. Some reporters blamed Beckham for England's loss and ultimate elimination from the tournament. So British fans devised a fitting punishment for the

Midfielders stay involved with offense, defense, and more. U.S. national team midfielder Julie Foudy used her soccer smarts as an analyst for World Cup 1998 TV broadcasts on ESPN.

midfielder. When the regular season resumed a month later, fans planned on waving 10,000 red cards from the stands as a reminder.

French midfielder Zinedine Zidane starred in the World Cup 1998 championship game against Brazil. "Zizou" debuted internationally as a 21-year-old substitute in 1994, ramming in two goals against the Czech Republic to save France with a 2–2 tie.

But Zidane suffered a fate similar to that of England's Beckham in 1998. After a red-card ejection for stomping a Saudi Arabian opponent at the beginning of World Cup play, Zidane was suspended for the next two games and couldn't return until the quarter-finals.

Once back, however, he made the difference for the French. Ukrainian coach Igor Lobanovsky raved to reporters about Zidane's leadership for the French. "He does everything you should expect from a soccer star of the 21st century," the coach said. "He helps the team first and himself next."

The dreaded red-card penalty—an "award" in soccer that no one wants!

5 PROTECT AND DEFEND

Some call them halfbacks. Most call them defenders. Many call them tough.

Defenders defend. Get the ball, stop the scorer—that's their assignment. Usually played four per team, three defenders will be joined by a "sweeper," who helps any defensive teammate. At times, a sweeper can seem like an assistant goalkeeper, the last defensive hope stationed in front of the net.

Defenders need to play zone or man-to-man. Although they don't get as much applause as scorers, defenders are mentioned first in game plans. When numbers are listed for a formation, such as 4–4–2, the numbers mean the team will line up in three levels on the field: 4 defenders, 4 midfielders, and 2 forwards.

"Marking," the term for guarding an opposing player, is a job for all defenders. Using their bodies as shields, defenders try to force offensive players away from the goal, or to the sidelines. No way but out—of bounds!—is the ultimate choice that defenders give a closely marked player.

Tackling has a different aim in soccer than in American football. A soccer tackle occurs when a defender slides feet-first on the ground to take the ball away from the dribbler. No foul is called even if physical contact occurs, as long as the referee feels that the defender was going for the ball and not for downing an opponent.

Tricking Tacklers

The best tackles have more than speed. Tackles need surprise and timing. Failing to make a tackle takes a defender out of position, which may hurt the defender's team but not the opponent: Players can easily dribble around or over an unsuccessful tackler.

A final challenge awaits the successful tackler involved in a clean collision: The offensive player who got upended may turn out to be a great actor. Faking injury sometimes helps get a foul called against the defender. This was especially true as the 1990s drew to a close. Referees at the time were trying to help create higher-scoring games by protecting offenses. More and more defenders were getting called for infractions such as tugging an opponent's jersey, or use of the hands.

What made soccer a favorite sport for C. J. Brown, Chicago Fire defender? "I liked having 11 people on the field and everybody playing all the time. Even if I didn't have the ball there was something to do. I wasn't just standing there, like in [American] football."

A well-executed tackle is an effective defensive move.

Freeing Up the Defense

Franz Beckenbauer is credited with revolutionizing the role of defenders. The West German star was given permission by coach Helmut Schon to roam freely on the field. Some say that the way Beckenbauer swept away balls from opponents resulted in today's term, "sweeper." Other teams adopted the Italian term *libero*, meaning "free player"— free to play anywhere on the field.

Sweeper was the ideal position for Norbert "Nobby" Stiles, a Manchester United regular from 1960 to 1971. His nickname was a takeoff on his first name. The 5-foot-7, 140-pounder was more than a sweeper. He was a magnet. When Stiles "marked" foes, he created space and time for strikers Bobby Charlton and Bobby Moore to score. Yet, surprisingly, Stiles was often described in the press as a player of limited physical talent and questionable passing skills.

Defender Eddie Pope was a major reason that D.C. United owned two MLS championships. Pope himself earned the league's player of the year award in 1997. But Pope's speed and magnetic man-to-man defense as a "marking back" weren't the only reasons he gained raves in the soccer world. Pope kept a reputation as one of the sport's cleanest defensemen.

"You have to be patient, and that is hard for a lot of defenders, even for me," he explained. "If you're going against a good forward, you can't just dive in." When the 24-year-old drew a red card in a 1998 MLS contest, it was his first ejection since high school.

> French defender Laurent Blanc was faked out of the 1998 World Cup final. In the semifinal versus Croatia, a Croatian defender pretended to hold his face in pain during a shoving spat with Blanc. The referee saw Blanc's flying arms, the Croatian's reaction, and assumed a fistfight. The red-card ejection included suspension.

Mental Muscle

Chicago Fire head coach Bob Bradley echoed Pope's defensive attitudes, while pointing to his own defender, C. J. Brown, as an example of how the position should be played.

Defender C. J. Brown (left), playing for the Chicago Fire, beats Ryan Tinsley of the Wizards to the ball.

"Some people had made [Brown] out to be purely a physical, strong defender. But I saw it a little bit different," Bradley said. "Obviously, he is physical and has good speed. But more than that, I saw he had excellent concentration. C. J. is very alert and good at timing tackles. He does real well at beating players to the ball, and he does it without fouling and overcommitting." Bradley went on, "I disagree with those who make him out to be overly physical, because he's done it for the most part this year [1998] without accumulating yellow cards. In order to play against top players and handle them in that way, you have to have other very, very good defensive qualities, which C. J. has."

Tottenham Hotspurs team captain Gary Mabbutt retired in 1999 after playing for the same team for 17 seasons. A dedicated defender, he overcame numerous injuries and played his entire career with diabetes.

Defenders defend. Get the ball, stop the scorer. The job often isn't easy, and sometimes it isn't pretty.

Defender Gary Mabbutt, team captain for the Tottenham Hotspurs, played for the same team for 17 seasons before announcing his retirement in 1999. During his career, Mabbutt once took only three months off after suffering a smashed cheekbone and eyesocket from a rival's elbow. He played wearing a mask to protect his facial wounds upon his return. Later, a snapped shinbone sidelined Mabbutt for a whole season before finally, at age 37, he was unable to recover from a knee injury.

Great tackles only seem to be one-on-one battles. A defender needs to have a teammate nearby, so that the ball-holder will remain covered even if the tackle fails. Also, a second defender should be near to get control of the ball and start a counterattack.

But Mabbutt remains a profile in courage for all defenders and all athletes. He played his entire career with diabetes, taking an insulin injection before every game, battling his own body while he battled other teams.

Fearless and inspiring, the best defenders defend their teams. When defenders combine attitude and action, they've found the winning game plan.

6 A GOALKEEPER'S GOALS

Goalkeepers don't count.

At least, when a coach says the team is playing a "4–3–3" or "4–4–2" formation, only defenders, midfielders, and forwards are counted in the mix. Everyone assumes the goalie will remain in the penalty area, minding his or her net.

True, a goalkeeper's job is to keep watch over a goal, 24 feet across and 8 feet high, stopping incoming shots that can travel up to 80 miles per hour. But a goalkeeper can also be an extra defender if needed. A goalie can even start a team's offense rolling, providing that the keeper keeps watch over the *entire* field and *all* the players!

Soccer rules state that a goalkeeper can play the ball with any part of the body, without interference from offensive players. But that does not stop attackers from playing mind games with goalies, getting as close as possible without making contact. After a team finally scores in a close contest, an opponent might briefly invade the goal and spike the ball into the net a second time, not for a point but for defiant celebration.

A goalie who strikes back isn't unheard of. In the 1994 match between Norway and Italy, Gianluca Pagliuca became the first goalkeeper in World Cup history to be ejected. Pagliuca was red-carded for flattening Norway's Oyvind Leonhardsen. As the old saying goes, too close for comfort?

Newer fans sometimes think that a goal-keeper who makes the most dives and leaps is the most talented. Actually, goalies caught out of position are often the ones who need frantic gymnastics to recover. An in-the-know keeper, who studies foes and knows which way the ball bounces, can do the job with less movement. Some play harder, some play smarter.

Watching an attacker's foot can help goalies anticipate a shot. But simply seeing an oncoming ball may not help. The "banana kick" is a nightmare for some goalies. This curving

Goalie Kasey Keller stretches to block a shot on goal in a match against Holland.

shot is made by kicking a ball with the instep of the foot, giving the ball a boomeranging sidespin that can be as confusing to grab as—well, a flying banana?

Playing for Keepers

Rules state that a goalkeeper must wear a different-colored jersey than his or her teammates and the other team. This way, opponents won't be tricked by 10 other players camping out inside the penalty box. But this doesn't mean that a goalie won't make any surprise appearances during the game. Veteran Major League Soccer goalkeeper Jorge Campos sometimes ranges to midfield to show off his foot skills even though a goalie can't use his hands outside the penalty area. And, like any show of power, there is a chance the move could cause trouble: Allowing a goal on an open, unminded net is one of soccer's biggest embarrassments, to a goalie and his or her team.

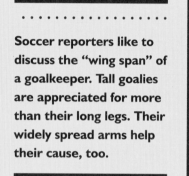

Soccer reporters like to discuss the "wing span" of a goalkeeper. Tall goalies are appreciated for more than their long legs. Their widely spread arms help their cause, too.

Balls bouncing off the side posts or crossbar of the net can remain in play. The best goalkeepers are masters of snagging such balls. A ball off the crossbar can be one of the most difficult for a keeper to field—a scare in the sky. Deflected straight up, the ball may seem to the goalie to float back down as lazily as a leaf. To the offense, however, the reduced speed of the ball is a perfect opportunity for an easy head-in score.

As the 1990s ended, goalkeepers were handling the ball less due to changes in the "back-pass" rule. For years, defenders who felt helpless with the ball could pass the ball back to the goalie. The goalie, protected in the penalty box, could take time and throw the ball to create an all-new play. Today's newer rules keep goalies from using their hands on a back-pass play.

Yikes! It's "Schmikes"!

Goalie Peter Schmeichel was known as "The Great Dane." In 1992 the 6-foot-4-inch goalkeeper helped Denmark win the European team championship. Later, his presence transformed Manchester United.

Daryl Ngan, an 18-year-old fan, described Schmeichel's success.

"There was an aura around him. Strikers are almost *afraid* of him when they're one on one with 'Schmikes,'" Ngan said.

Ngan recalled one special match he witnessed that proved the star goalie's worth, a 1996 matchup against league rival Newcastle, which included three special stops. Three minutes after the game started, Schmeichel hit the ground to smother a shot like a blanket. Two minutes later, an attacker came within five yards. Schmeichel's long arms stopped that shot, too.

"The third one was the most crucial," Ngan said. "It was late in the second half, and there was a scramble in the Man U box. The ball dropped at Robert Lee's feet, and he tried to shoot round Pete. It looked as if Newcastle was going to draw level when suddenly Schmikes stretched himself and got hold of the ball. The sigh of unbelief and the applause afterward from the Newcastle fans proved how good that stop was."

As an amateur footballer himself, Ngan has special reason to study his hero. "Pete once said in an interview that the reason [for] his success was practice, practice and practice," Ngan said. "He also mentioned self-confidence, belief in oneself. He believed that he is the best. That I believe is the difference between him and other keepers . . . very high self-confidence." Ngan added, "Being a keeper myself, I also see that as the most important element in goalkeeping: belief in my own ability."

Popular goalie Peter Schmeichel, playing for Manchester United, enjoys cheers from the crowd after stopping a shot on goal in a game against Newcastle.

GAME PLAN IN ACTION

7

When successful soccer players are described, the adjectives often get physical:

Fastest

Tallest

Strongest

Fans sometimes describe their favorite soccer stars in almost magical terms, saying there is no way to explain how the player manages to be in the right place at the right time.

The explanation may be in a word often left out of tributes to fine players: "smart." At either end of the field, soccer game plans vary from moment to moment. Players need to think about many things at once. Just like a student with homework, a soccer player who studies gains an advantage.

Better to Give Than Receive

For more than a decade, center forward Emilio Butragueño's offense lit up professional leagues in Spain and Mexico. He was known as "The Vulture," for swooping on balls with lightning reaction.

Was it only speed? Hardly. "Before receiving the ball, you need to know exactly the position of your teammates in order to gain time. Time is very important," Butragueño said. "Before touching the ball, you should

England won the 1966 World Cup with a strategy called the "penguin system." Like the flightless birds, the English formation worked without "wings" in their offense! England beat West Germany. The game was watched on television by more than 400 million viewers.

know exactly when and where you are going to pass the ball. In that sense, the defense can't predict what you are going to do. The ideal would be to think before receiving the ball and act when you have it instead of receiving. By thinking and acting, it will save a step and save 1-2 seconds, which is essential in soccer. One or two plays can decide a game. This is very important, and [so is] any player who has this ability. In the last 40 meters in front of the goal, that quality becomes more important."

Expect the Unexpected

In the first round of the Women's World Cup game between the United States and China in 1995, shock came after just six minutes of play. USA striker Michelle Akers prepared to defend a Chinese corner kick. She leaped to head off the approaching ball. Meanwhile, a Chinese player keeping her eye on the ball didn't keep an eye on Akers. She snapped her torso forward, wanting to win the header race against the American star.

Akers headed first. But Akers paid for it when she also fielded her Chinese foe's forehead in the back of her own head. In addition to instant unconsciousness, Akers twisted her right knee as she hit the ground.

At age 33, Akers was America's oldest player on the 1999 Women's World Cup championship squad. Versus China in the final, she found more bad luck. As both teams neared the 90th minute still scoreless, Akers fell to the ground—again. She was

"Play on" means that the referee will ignore a foul. Why? Suppose, in mid-attack, a defender trips you. After falling, you recover, and you and the ball still find the goal. Calling the foul would have stopped the score and harmed the fouled team twice.

helped from the field and did not return to the game.

At first, reporters guessed that heat exhaustion was the cause. Others suspected she had been punched by a Chinese foe. Each answer was partly correct. When American goalkeeper Briana Scury knocked away China's corner kick, Akers was in the way.

No More Rehearsal

Soccer rules ask players to use their feet and to use their heads. But hands are all right for an in-bounds pass following an out-of-bounds ball. And defenders who don't regroup quickly may get hoodwinked by fast-thinking offenses.

On free kicks, corner kicks, and throw-ins, an offense often uses a "set piece," a rehearsed play much like that of an American football team. The best defense against a set piece seems to be combination marking. The defense may choose one striker for man-to-man coverage, while other defenders assume zone positions, watching for runs on goal.

Who's Laughing Now?

The eyes have it.

A player who reads an opponent's face too closely can be faked out. The surest defense is to watch the chest of a player trying to move the ball. Everything else—

Kristine Lilly keeps her eye on the ball as she prepares to head it. This is a legal maneuver, but it can occasionally result in a collision when more than one player attempts to head the ball at the same time.

eyes, hips, hands, and feet—can lure and deceive any defender out of position.

Fakery can work both ways. During the European Cup final in 1984, Zimbabwe goalkeeper Bruce Grobbelaar tried a shaky-kneed dance routine and even handstands to distract Italian foes.

Cut the Bicycles

Some soccer players struggle to do it right. Some fans struggle to say it right.

The "scissors kick" and the "bicycle kick" are different moves! The two terms are not interchangeable. Pelé and other scorers favor the bicycle kick for a booming surprise, performing a near-somersault to launch a kick over the shoulder.

The scissors kick is a more modest move, less used when trying for goals. Here, a player leaps, opening and closing the legs like the blades on a scissors. The ball is kicked in the direction the player faces, though the player leans sideways in the air.

Sometimes, strategy is out the window as both teams are surprised by what unfolds on the field. England's 18-year-old forward Michael Owen scored what reporters voted as "The Goal" of World Cup 1998. Owen dribbled through 50 yards of Argentinean defenders, a one-man scoring explosion.

Going It Alone

Although the best soccer players find success by keeping things simple, one of the simplest-looking parts of the game haunts many players.

The penalty kick is one-on-one soccer: the kicker versus goalkeeper. The penalty shootout occurs after an overtime period fails to untie a tied game.

Argentina goalkeeper Carlos Roa told of pressure on the other end of the penalty kick. "In a shootout, you must forget everything else and think only of stopping the shot," he has said. "You are not expected to stop it. But if you do, you can win."

A bicycle kick (left) sends the ball back over the shoulder of the kicker. A scissors kick (right) sends the ball in the direction the kicker is facing.

Gary Lineker, captain of England's national team, is famed both for a successful penalty kick in the 1990 World Cup against Cameroon—and for his later recounting of the play. As he has told it:

"[I felt] relief at hearing the referee's whistle, thinking we could be back in the game [after trailing 2–1]. Then, it dawned on me—I was the one expected to take the kick! I must confess I had some other thoughts, negative thoughts. Will they allow me back in the country [if I miss]?"

Lineker went on: "Then I thought, 'Get a grip. *Think about what you are going to do with it. Concentrate. Don't think of anything else.*' I concentrated on where I was going to put it, and hoped the goalie went the other way. Even if I missed it, we were still in the game."

Lineker's game plan? "If I hit in the middle [of the goal], I thought he'd dive out of the way, if he does the same thing [as he's done earlier in the game]. I wasn't sure which way he'd go, but I was sure he'd go early again." And, Lineker finished, "That's the way it worked out."

Do It Simply, Do It Well

Claudio Reyna, a member of the 1998 U.S. national team, agrees with those who call soccer "the simple game."

"If you look at a high-level soccer game, the moves are mostly very simple," he has said. "It's a matter of practicing the ones that are your bread and butter. I don't do that many tricks. I just practice two or three. That's all that you will need to get out of most situations."

Just being on the field might be the key game plan for top players. Teofilo Cubillas, who debuted in 1970, scored 10 goals while playing in three World Cups for Peru. Yet, he saw his greatest feat as something different. "I never got a red card," he said with pride. "I was never expelled from the game."

Most successful members of the sport agree that soccer doesn't depend on magical moves. Bobby Moore, the team captain of England's 1966 World Cup winners, once said, "The secret of soccer is to do the simple things supremely well."

THE WORLD COMES HOME

8

Was the 1998 World Cup a done deal before the first match was played?

France was hosting the tournament. The national team had a home-field advantage on its side. But the French team's recent history was shaky at best.

West Germany had defeated France in the 1982 and 1986 World Cup finals. After that, France failed to even qualify for the 1990 or 1994 tournaments. And only being the host country had guaranteed France its spot in 1998.

Worry for fans didn't end there. Paris resident and fan Christophe Meynet said, "[My] hope was dimmed after looking at the French roster. France's national team coach, Aimé Jacquet, was second-guessed in his choice for the selection." The roster did not include David Ginola or Eric Cantona, "two excellent players who played in the English league."

The final blow came when France's major airline threatened a strike that would stop all flights just before the tournament began. For a few tense days, France wondered if the world would even be able to come to the World Cup.

As the strike settled down and the world began to gather in France, fans like Meynet began to focus, once again, on the game. He sounded hopeful, but realistic. "I thought that, as usual, it [would be the] great nations of football—Brazil, Argentina, Italy, or Germany—who would win World Cup 98, because they're strong teams," Meynet said.

But like any true fan, Meynet hoped. "Maybe there would be a surprise with the Netherlands or France as challengers," he said. It seemed possible, especially since "France was in a relatively easy group for the first round." French fans were sure their team would get to the second round. But after that, Meynet said, "the history of World Cups shows that France was not able to win against Italy or Germany in semifinals." Still—"We all dreamed of a victory, because it was in France. [We] really thought it was possible."

French fans wondered and worried about their team, often called *Les Bleus* because of its team color. Likewise, the players wondered and worried about their fans. High ticket prices were keeping average fans from attending. France team captain Didier Deschamps complained, "People come to the park like it's a play. It annoys me. When we came on the field, we saw people wearing dark suits, as if they'd come to a funeral. That is not in the World Cup's spirit."

Inside the stadium or out, French fans rooted as their team survived match after match, climbing to a semifinal match against Croatia, a team filled with underdog appeal and universal fan support. France's 2–1 win came at unexpected hands. Defender Lillian Thuram produced both goals, even though he hadn't scored in 36 previous games for the nationals.

The semifinals were over—and France was still alive. "We all dreamed of a victory, because it was in France," Meynet had said. Could it actually be possible now?

The Stade de France was packed with fans for the 1998 World Cup final on July 12, 1998.

The Impossible Dream

The last team France would face was the defending champion, Brazil, which had qualified for *every* World Cup since the tournament was born in 1930. France would go to this final battle without sweeper Laurent Blanc, who was suspended for a red card drawn in a shoving match with a Croatian defender. Blanc's absence meant two French starters would need to adjust by playing new positions. But defender Thuram shrugged off the shift, telling reporters, "If you approach the game with the right attitude, you can play any position."

Blanc was still able to help France's game plan, even from the bench. For Blanc had once been on a professional team in Spain, along with current Brazilian star Ronaldo. As a teammate, Blanc had learned that Ronaldo tended to move left while dribbling. Blanc told his replacement, Frank Leboeuf, about Ronaldo's weakness. Throughout the final match, Leboeuf would haunt Ronaldo on the pitch.

World Cup history is filled with upsets, with "can't-lose" teams that lost. One of the biggest shocks ever came when the USA beat England, 1–0, in the first round of the 1950 World Cup. Bettors gave 3-to-1 odds for the English to win the Cup, putting America at 500-to-1.

French midfielder Zinedine Zidane, after suffering his own first-round tantrum and red card, had returned to the field but not to top playing form. French media nicknamed him "The Black Cat" because of his bad luck and poor showings in earlier tournaments.

Bad luck? More than 80,000 fans in Stade de France and a television audience of more than two billion saw Zidane head in the first goal at the game's 27-minute mark—a feat that Zidane repeated just before the first half ended.

Didier Deschamps was another good-luck charm for the French team. His short passes were never dazzling. Yet he became a dependable transition as France worked its way from defense to offense.

In the 1998 World Cup final against Brazil, midfielder Zidane scored France's first goal with a header.

Emmanuel Petit capped the French finish. Even with a 2–0 lead, Pettit put on a burst of speed in the game's final minute for one last goal, creating a Cup-winning shutout.

The Other Side of the World

Not since 1958 had a World Cup championship been decided by such a large margin. French forwards had even missed several scoring chances, including some seemingly clear shots. Had only fate prevented a six- or seven-goal blowout?

Perhaps. But most fans were ready to blame problems suffered by young superstar Ronaldo. The 21-year-old Brazilian, dubbed "the world's greatest player" by the international media, managed just three shots for the whole game. What went wrong?

The manager of the Paris hotel where the Brazilian team stayed helped unravel part of the mystery. Hotel workers learned that Ronaldo suffered a seizure the afternoon of the game. Some reports said the star nearly swallowed his tongue during the collapse, and could have choked himself.

Four games earlier, Ronaldo had injured an ankle. The medication he had been taking could have caused the convulsion. But Ronaldo's roommate, Roberto Carlos, didn't know what was happening. When Roberto collapsed, Carlos screamed for help. The whole team came running. Panicked, they tried to find medical help for their teammate.

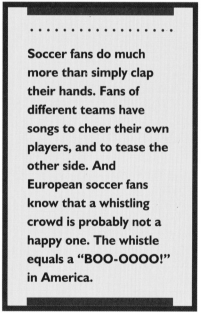

Soccer fans do much more than simply clap their hands. Fans of different teams have songs to cheer their own players, and to tease the other side. And European soccer fans know that a whistling crowd is probably not a happy one. The whistle equals a "BOO-OOOO!" in America.

Ronaldo was taken for a hospital checkup before the game. He had, by now, recovered. He passed his physical exam with no problem. But in the meantime, following World Cup rules, both coaches had submitted their lineups for the game. When the lineups were announced, shock spread when fans learned that Brazil didn't intend to play Ronaldo. But after the young star's checkup, FIFA ignored its own rule. The ruling body allowed Ronaldo to be added to the lineup less than one hour before the game.

Where were the Brazilian players before the game? No one saw a pregame practice. That's because the team remained in its dressing room. Arguments flared over whether Ronaldo should play or not. Assistant coach Zico led the disapproval. Worrying over the health of Ronaldo, how could Brazil focus on any game plan? Was Ronaldo really healthy enough to focus past all this tension? To help the young star, the team doctor gave Ronaldo a

France beat Brazil 3–0 to take the World Cup for the first time.

tranquilizer just before the game—but neglected to tell the coach about it.

Later, Roberto Carlos told reporters, "Today, I can say we lost the Cup at 2 o'clock that Sunday afternoon, because until that moment, the thought of losing the *penta* [the fifth Cup] had not crossed our minds." It surely had not crossed Carlos's mind. Just two days before, Carlos had told the press, "At this moment, our team has no weaknesses."

Brazil had been champions before. They would, someday, be champions again. But today, World Cup glory had come home. A Frenchman, Jules Rimet, had organized the first World Cup tournament in 1930. The first cup was given his name. After Brazil won the Cup a third time in 1970, the award was given permanently to that team. But this "new" 11-pound gold trophy had no reason to leave the country.

At least, not for four more years. Or maybe even longer, depending on the next French game plan.

GLOSSARY

advantage rule   the rule that a referee can ignore a foul and call "play on" if stopping play might harm the fouled team more.

backs   another name for defenders who play in the rear, in front of the goalkeeper. The term includes the left and right fullbacks as well as the centerbacks, which some call sweepers.

banana kick   a kick with a strong curve.

bicycle kick   a kick performed with the body horizontal in midair and directing the ball over the head. Brazil star Pelé perfected the move. Not to be confused with the scissors kick.

booked   a player's name that is noted by a referee for a yellow- or red-card infraction.

boots   soccer shoes with cleats.

cap   an award to players who appear in a game for their national team. Once, players received actual caps after such an appearance.

center   to pass the ball from the wings, or sides of the field, into the penalty area. Also known as a cross.

center forward   a striker leading the offensive attack.

center half midfielder   the midfield's playmaker.

chip   a high, arcing shot meant to stay over the heads of defenders or goalkeeper.

clear   to kick the ball out of the defense's penalty area or space where a goal could be likely.

corner kick a free kick by an attacking player from a corner of the field. A corner kick occurs any time a defender touches the ball before it crosses all the way over the end line.

dangerous play any action deemed by a referee likely to cause an injury. The player whistled for dangerous play is always penalized with at least a yellow card. Some will get a red card.

direct free kick an unopposed kick awarded because of a personal foul, such as pushing, holding, tripping, or kicking. The kick is taken from the spot of the foul.

dropped ball in cases when play stops for reasons besides a foul (such as an injury), the referee drops the ball onto the ground between two opposing players to restart the game

flank the wing sides of the field.

friendly an exhibition game, usually between national teams. The outcome won't alter team standings.

goal when someone scores; whenever the ball crosses the entire goal line, a goal is scored.

goal area a rectangle-shaped space, 60 feet wide by 18 feet deep in front of each goal.

goalkeeper the only player who can handle the ball within the penalty area with his or her hands. Also known as a goalie, this person protects the goal against scorers.

goal kick the defense takes this free kick after the offensive team has knocked the ball out of bounds over the end line.

goal lines lines running from corner flag to corner flag across each end of the field of play where the goal is positioned, marking the end of the playing area at the far end of each side of the field.

goals two wooden or metal posts, 24 feet apart, and a crossbar, 8 feet high, are backed by a net in the center of the goal lines.

golden goal a "first goal wins" way of breaking a tied game in overtime, instead of playing an entire overtime period. Used by some international soccer tournaments, such as the World Cup.

half either of two periods, 45 minutes each, constituting a game.

halfbacks another name for midfielders.

handball a foul called when a player other than a goalkeeper intentionally plays a ball with the hand. Within the penalty area, a penalty shot is awarded. A direct free kick is awarded if the goalkeeper touches the ball outside the penalty area. Handball is a major violation.

hat trick one player scoring three goals in one game.

header a shot or pass with the head.

indirect free kick an unopposed kick award because of a minor foul at the spot where the foul occurred. A player besides the kicker must touch the ball before it can become a goal.

infraction the breaking of a rule.

libero Italian for "free player." Another term for sweeper.

linesman either of two officials who stay outside the touchlines to signal if a ball is out of play or to call offsides.

marking the close guarding of a player from the other team.

match a British term for a game. A match runs 90 minutes, with a 12-minute break between each 45-minute half.

midfielders players lined up in the middle of a team's field half, in front of defenders but behind forwards. Midfielders are a connection between offensive and defensive play.

offside an infraction in which an attacker sends a pass to a teammate without two defenders (which can include a goalkeeper) between the teammate and the goal.

offside trap a defensive plan that rushes defensive players forward, so as to catch an attacking player offside.

penalty area a 60-foot wide by 18-foot deep rectangle in front of each goal, where the goalkeeper can use his or her hands.

penalty kick a free kick awarded because of a personal foul or for the intentional handling of the ball by a defending player within the penalty area. The penalty kick must occur 12 yards from the goal line in the center of the penalty area, with only the goalkeeper defending the shot.

pitch British term for the playing field, a rectangle measuring between 100 and 130 yards in length and 50 to 100 yards in width. For the World Cup and international matches, rules require a pitch of 110 to 120 yards long and 70 to 80 yards wide.

red card   the card shown to a player being ejected from a match by the referee. An ejected player cannot be replaced. Red-carded players can be forced to sit out additional matches.

referee   the only on-field official who enforces the rules of the game, while keeping game time. A referee has the power to eject a player from the game for fouls or bad behavior.

save   the prevention of a score by a goalkeeper. Saves come by knocking the ball away from the goal or catching it.

scissors kick   a kick in which a player leaps and thrusts the legs apart, much like blades on a scissors. The ball is kicked in the direction the player is facing, a side volley of sorts.

shootout   the answer to tied or scoreless games. In Major League Soccer and other North American leagues, the shootout is a one-on-one. An attacker 35 yards away has to dribble and score against the opposing goalkeeper. In the World Cup or international matches, penalty kicks take the form of shootouts. In Major League Soccer, the shootout happens at the end of a regular game. Internationally, the shootout comes after the overtime period.

slide tackle   sliding into the ball and knocking it away from a foe. If the tackler hits the attacker's legs before the ball, a penalty is called. An incorrect slide tackle can result in a red- or yellow-card penalty.

soccer ball   official ball; 27–28 inches around and 14–16 ounces in weight.

stoppage time   time added to the end of either half by the referee to make up for time lost due to injuries or other delays during each half. Only the referee can decide how much stoppage time can be awarded. Also called injury time.

strikers   forwards or attackers, seen as a team's biggest scoring threats.

sweeper   a defender who roams behind the back four with no marking job. An assistant goalkeeper of sorts, a sweeper helps out on offense and defense.

throw-in   the restart of play after the ball has crossed the touchlines. A throw-in is given to the opponents of the team that last touched the ball before it went out of play.

touch lines   the lines running the full length of the field on each side of the playing area. Also called sidelines.

trapping   the use of any legal part of the body to control a ball from the air to the ground.

volley   striking a ball still in the air to attempt a shot or pass.

wall   the line of players used to oppose a direct kick, lined up 10 yards away.

wingers   players on the left or right side of the offense, remaining close to the touchline, helping forwards and midfielders.

yellow card   a card of caution shown by a referee to a player called for a dangerous play foul. A red card and automatic ejection comes when the same player in the same match receives a second yellow card. In some leagues and tournaments, players getting yellow cards in consecutive games or matches can be made to sit out one game.

For More Information

Books

Gifford, Clive. *The Usborne Soccer School: Tactics.* London: Usborne Publishing Ltd., 1997.

Lineker, Gary. *The Young Soccer Player.* London: Dorling Kindersley Ltd., 1994.

Ominsky, Dave and P. J. Haari. *Soccer Made Simple: A Spectator's Guide.* Los Angeles: First Base Sports, Inc., 1994.

Stewart, Peter. *Way to Play Soccer.* Rocklin, CA: Prima Publishing, 1995.

Woog, Dan. *The Ultimate Soccer Almanac.* Los Angeles: Lowell House Juvenile, 1998.

Books for Older Readers

Cantor, Andres with Daniel Arcucci. *Goooal! A Celebration of Soccer.* New York: Simon and Schuster, 1996.

Clarkson, Wensley. *Ronaldo! 21 Years of Genius and 90 Minutes That Shook the World.* London: Blake Publishing, 1998.

Davies, Pete. *Twenty-Two Foreigners in Funny Shorts: The Intelligent Fan's Guide to Soccer and World Cup '94.* New York: Random House, 1994.

Gardner, Paul. *The Simplest Game: The Intelligent Fan's Guide to the World of Soccer.* New York: Macmillan, 1996.

Internet Resources

www.fifa.com
The organization in charge of soccer. Search here for World Cup tidbits.

www.mslnet.com
Major League Soccer has an official site.

www.womensoccer.com
"Women's Soccer World" magazine's site gives a great overview on both professional and amateur levels of the sport for women.

www.soccertv.com
Games from all over the world may be on your television. The trick is to learn the time and channel. Start here.

www.spaceports.com/~mprais/futbr/index
"Brazil, the Land of Football." How does Brazil remain a World Cup power? Visit this impressive fan-made site for answers.

INDEX

Page numbers in *italics* refer to illustrations.